Finding Strength

A DEVOTIONAL BIBLE STUDY

NICOLE ALVILLAR

TRILOGY
PROFESSIONAL PUBLISHING MEETS POWERFUL PROMOTION
A wholly owned subsidiary of TBN

Trilogy Christian Publishers

A Wholly Owned Subsidiary of Trinity Broadcasting Network

2442 Michelle Drive | Tustin, CA 92780

Copyright © 2024 by Nicole Alvillar

All Scripture quotations, unless otherwise noted, taken from THE HOLY BIBLE, NEW INTERNATIONAL VERSION®, NIV® Copyright © 1973, 1978, 1984, 2011 by Biblica, Inc.® Used by permission. All rights reserved worldwide. Scripture quotations marked NKJV are taken from the New King James Version®. Copyright © 1982 by Thomas Nelson. Used by permission. All rights reserved.

Scripture quotations marked ESV are taken from the ESV® Bible (The Holy Bible, English Standard Version®), copyright © 2001 by Crossway Bibles, a publishing ministry of Good News Publishers. Used by permission. All rights reserved.

All rights reserved, including the right to reproduce this book or portions thereof in any form whatsoever.

For information, address Trilogy Christian Publishing

Rights Department, 2442 Michelle Drive, Tustin, CA 92780.

Trilogy Christian Publishing/ TBN and colophon are trademarks of Trinity Broadcasting Network.

For information about special discounts for bulk purchases, please contact Trilogy Christian Publishing.

Trilogy Disclaimer: The views and content expressed in this book are those of the author and may not necessarily reflect the views and doctrine of Trilogy Christian Publishing or the Trinity Broadcasting Network.

10 9 8 7 6 5 4 3 2 1

Library of Congress Cataloging-in-Publication Data is available.

ISBN 979-8-89597-096-6 | ISBN 979-8-89597-097-3 (ebook)

Preface

During Covid-19, when we were on lockdown and I was working from home, as I'm sure many of you were as well, I began to feel restless or uneasy spiritually. I serve in church on the worship team and at the time my husband and I led a young adult ministry, and during Covid it felt like everything was taken away. Yes, we continued to meet via online meetings, but it wasn't the same. My heart was heavy, and I knew many people were feeling disconnected and fearful about what was happening in the world. We did not know how long the lockdown would continue, and life was held in the balance. I asked God what I should do, and I felt led to start having online Bible studies through Zoom and Teams with my coworkers, with the young adult women church group, and with my family. Finding strength developed as a topic out of these Bible studies to encourage us to keep moving forward, and trusting in the Lord that He would get us through one of the most difficult trials and seasons that we were all experiencing together. From there, these were integrated into short devotions with a Bible study component to reflect, meditate, and pray on God's Word.

Devotion 1
THE SOURCE OF STRENGTH

Life can be compared to a series of changing seasons. Some seasons remind us of spring and summer, and others like fall and winter. In the natural, we expect the seasons to change but don't always know when the change will happen. Sometimes we get a long, hot summer, and sometimes we get a long, harsh winter. Our experiences in life, whether good or bad, leave lasting marks on our hearts, and we can remember how long it felt and how difficult it was to come through. Hopefully, after the season has passed, we can at least find ourselves a little wiser and stronger from it, but there are times when we are broken down and at the end of our rope because of how harsh it was.

It's uncertain how quickly life will come, but when life is "good," we can forget to cherish the moment, and when life is "not good," we seem to feel time passes too slowly. During the season of sunshine and rainbows, we feel strong and able to accomplish our goals, but in the other season, we feel depleted and uncertain which direction to move in. This is not an uncommon scenario, and yet we are never really prepared for it or question why and how it happened. We have become accustomed to living in a world where we have easy access to every kind of resource, and without much effort on our part, a solution can be found. The trouble comes when life events not in our control come, or our poor choices lead us to bad places we know are not good, and we need help. A quick search is not going to give us a solution, and it's going to take time and effort on our part to make it through. In these moments we find ourselves feeling incapable of making any kind of decision, and we don't have the resources, knowledge, and information on how to begin. Trials that affect our lifestyle, family, and friends can leave us feeling blindsided, unsteady, lost, insecure, heartbroken, and anxious. These are life-changing events that place us at a turning point where decisions need to be made, but the strength to make them is not there.

Our history of "how-to," with all the tools, resources, and information we have access to is not enough this time, so therefore, we feel inadequate to move forward with any decision. Our self-centered world has not taught us how to draw strength from others, how to lean on others, or most importantly, how to draw strength and lean on God. Jesus tells us in John 16:33 (NKJV), "In the world you will have tribulation; but be of good cheer,

I have overcome the world." He is a God of a limitless supply of all we could ever need, and yet we try to live life without Him—and most importantly, without Him as our first choice when we need help. God is not supposed to be a last resort; He is to be our first choice, our first option. Why should we look elsewhere, when the Word of God clearly states in Philippians 4:19 (NIV), "And my God will meet all your needs according to the riches of his glory in Christ Jesus." That means He already has the information, knowledge, and resources that we need to move forward. We must choose Him to be that one source for all we need and admit that we don't have all the answers, and neither does anyone else. We must recognize that we don't know it all, nor can we live and supply our own resources. We are weak in our own strength. We need help. We need a God who supplies all our needs. It benefits us to realize that we are not self-sufficient and all-knowing. When we accept this, it takes the pressure off us and moves us to a position of being able to receive and be saved from any trial that we are facing. In this place of humbling, we can release all responsibility of trying to make it happen on our own and draw on answers from an all-knowing God.

Deciding to accept God's help to save us is easy and moves Him to our first choice as a source for everything we need. The Word of God tells us, "Because, if you confess with your mouth that Jesus is Lord and believe in your heart that God raised him from the dead, you will be saved. For with the heart one believes and is justified, and with the mouth one confesses and is saved" (Romans 10:9-10 ESV). Believing that these scriptures are true and speaking them out is all you need to do to begin the journey toward making it through any season by depending on an Almighty God. It is in the recognition of who He is as Savior and Lord of our life that we position ourselves to receive His strength for all we need.

Devotion 1

BIBLE STUDY 1

We live in a self-centered world that has not taught us to lean on others, to draw strength from others, and worst of all, to draw strength from God. It is a "sink or swim" mentality that causes us to tread water, get tired, begin to sink, get just enough energy to come up for air, and tread more water. The cycle continues, and we become consumed with our personal circumstances and never move forward. This "sink or swim" mentality means our trials keep us so occupied that we have no energy to rise above them or help others around us. This method of trying it on our own makes us ineffective in our own lives and in others' lives.

DISCUSSION QUESTIONS

1. Where do you think we learned the concept to wait to do it on our own, and then if we can't, to go to God as a last resort?

2. If the Bible says God has all we need, then why don't we go to Him first?

3. How many times have you taken on the responsibility to be strong for everyone, and it wiped you out?

4. Can we recognize that if we made Jesus our first choice, things could be different?

5. How can we grow our relationship with Jesus and work on leaning and drawing on Him for our strength?

Devotion 1

DISCUSSION NOTES

Finding Strength

VERSE STUDY

John 16:33 (NKJV), "These things I have spoken to you, that in Me you may have peace. In the world you will have tribulation; but be of good cheer, I have overcome the world."

1. What does the word *tribulation* in this verse mean to you? _____

   _____

   _____

   _____

   _____

   _____

2. As you reflect and focus on these words that Jesus is speaking, take a moment and realize that He is speaking directly to you. He knows exactly what you are facing, and regardless of what it is, He is saying that He is your peace in this place. How does that make you feel? _____

   _____

   _____

   _____

   _____

   _____

3. Accepting Jesus as your Lord and Savior means more than just choosing to believe in Him. It means we receive His goodness even when we think we don't deserve it, and this brings us joy. Does choosing to "be of good cheer" because of what Jesus has done for you change the perspective you have of your circumstances? How? _____

_____

_____

_____

_____

_____

4. In this scripture, Jesus is encouraging us to look to Him for our source of joy and peace during trials and tribulations. If you can begin doing this on a daily basis, how do you see this improving your overall perspective and attitude toward future hardships? _____

_____

_____

_____

_____

SCRIPTURE REFERENCES

Proverbs 24:10 (NIV), "If you falter in a time of trouble, how small is your strength!"

Philippians 4:19 (NIV), "And my God will meet all your needs according to the riches of his glory in Christ Jesus."

Nehemiah 8:10 (NIV), "Do not grieve, for the joy of the Lord is your strength."

Psalm 28:8 (NIV), "The Lord is the strength of His people, a fortress of salvation for his anointed one."

Romans 10:9-10 (ESV), "Because, if you confess with your mouth that Jesus is Lord and believe in your heart that God raised him from the dead, you will be saved. For with the heart one believes and is justified, and with the mouth one confesses and is saved."

Devotion 1

CLOSING PRAYER

Father God, thank You for sending Your Son Jesus to die on the cross for me. I believe in my heart that You raised Jesus from the dead, and He is alive. Save me from my sin, forgive me, and make me a new creation. I position myself in Your love to receive all that You have for me; be my source of strength, because I know that I cannot do it on my own. I surrender all that I am to You and look to You to supply all my needs, according to Your riches in glory. Thank You for being my Provider, in Jesus' name. Amen.

Finding Strength

PERSONAL PRAYER NOTES

Devotion 2

PURSUING YOUR SOURCE

Every time we discover a way to get what we need, find a good deal, or discover a way to improve our situation, we will continue to use it. We also know how to use our gifts and talents to get what we want, and when we find a sure thing, we will continue to go there until it is no longer available. The good news is that God's supply is limitless! It states in His Word that He supplies all our needs, meaning He will never run out of what we need. God is always in the present. He is the same yesterday, today, and forever, which means He never changes who He is or what He can do! This good news brings life and truth to us. All we need to do is believe and act in faith that He will do it. This means taking one minute to one day at a time, trusting that God will provide what we need. It may take some time to learn to think this way, but it is a process that renews our minds. We have learned to be self-sufficient and now, we need to learn to be dependent on a God who many times and again tells us that He gives us strength. Isaiah 40:29-30 (NIV) tells us, "He gives strength to the weary and increases the power of the weak. Even youths grow tired and weary, and young men stumble and fall." These are encouraging words to us. He gives to those who are *weary*, which means "to be worn out in strength or energy; to be exhausted of patience, tolerance, or pleasure; or a state of being depleted naturally." Many things that occur in life can make us weary, whether it's from hardship, failure, misfortune, loss, or destruction. We have all felt weary for one reason or another and may continue to feel this way, because we are using our own strength, energy, patience, and know-how to pick ourselves up, only to find ourselves tired again. The scripture continues to say that even youths grow tired and weary, meaning age does not matter. We live in a world where evil and misfortune happen at any age. Age is not a luxury in life that excludes us when there is trauma or loss. Many times we hear, "Oh, they are young; they can handle it," but that is not true either. We are all susceptible to life, no matter the age, and we will grow tired and weary.

Weariness leads to a lack of concentration, motivation, and decision-making skills, with the result of a "stumble and fall" noted at the end of verse 30. When we hit a low state of weariness, we can easily make mistakes that lead to further destruction in our lives. This is a common theme and reality of the world we live in, but the answer is revealed in verse 31. "But those who hope in the

Lord will renew their strength. They will soar on wings like eagles; they will run and not grow weary, they will walk and not be faint" (Isaiah 40:31 NIV). This is good news and is everything we could ever want to get us out of the dark places we find ourselves in when we have no answers, and when we've done all we can and we think all is lost. We need to turn our focus from what we could have/should have, did do/didn't do, and put all our hope in the Lord. God is so good, because He speaks to us in steps. First, God tells us to put our hope in Him, then He will renew our strength. He makes it clear to us that once we have renewed strength, we will be able to soar on wings like eagles. Soar like eagles, above the circumstances, higher, where the air is clean and clear. This does not mean the circumstances have changed or disappeared, but we will not be pulled down into them as before. Being high above makes everything look small below; you are light and not weighed down by the pressures of life. This process may be slow, but as you continue to trust in the Lord that what He has said is true, you will begin to soar a little bit more each day.

To get that high up, all the burdens and luggage that we carry to show what we've been through must fall off. They cannot be taken with us to these heights because they cause us to be off balance, and too much attention to them will throw off our ability to soar. Many times, what makes us weary are the burdens of our loss, failures, heartache, and the expectations of others that we continue to put on, day in and day out. We end up wearing them as a badge of sympathy, despair, and regret, to explain why we feel and act the way we do. When we put our hope in the Lord, we choose to remove these burdens by letting Him take them. In Matthew 11:28-30 (NIV), Jesus tells us, "Come to me, all you who are weary and burdened, and I will give you rest. Take my yoke upon you and learn from me, for I am gentle and humble in heart, and you will find rest for your souls. For my yoke is easy and my burden is light." Jesus tells us to find rest, the answers to our cares, in Him. The natural answer to feeling tired and weary is rest. Our only place of true rest will be found in Jesus. Jesus gives us specific direction to exchange our burden for His yoke, which is light. What Jesus carries is not going to weigh us down or wear us out. It is meant to teach us how to live according to His ways, not ours; i.e., on wings like eagles. This is how we will learn how to run and not grow weary, because we aren't using our own strength. We will walk and not faint or be at a loss for direction or purpose. We will have strength and purpose that comes from our God of limitless supply, and we will soar in life.

Devotion 2

BIBLE STUDY 2

A *yoke* is what is placed on oxen to help plow a field. The yoke has three purposes:

1. It is used to attach the plow or the cart that is to be pulled (the burden, so to speak, that many of us carry)

2. It is where the oxen can be directed, guided from

3. It keeps the oxen connected to each other

Many times, without realizing it, we place the yoke of our worries, fears, failures, despair, loss, trials, and tribulations on daily and carry them around with us. We even do this after these circumstances have passed, but out of habit, choice, confession, right, or reason, or even as an excuse, we carry it. Jesus tells us this way of life is tiresome, heavy, labored, and difficult. We are not called to "pull our way through life." Instead, we are to take off this yoke and make an exchange with Jesus. We are to accept the yoke He has for us that will lead and guide us through our trials. His way of doing things is gentle, where we find rest from life's trials, because through Jesus we don't carry our mistakes, burdens, failures, or losses; instead, we come to Him and He exchanges them for mercy, grace, and the forgiveness of sin, and they are washed away.

DISCUSSION QUESTIONS

1. Can you recognize an area in your life where switching your focus and hope in the Lord is needed?

2. Are there some burdens that you may be carrying around that are weighing you down?

3. Are you ready to make an exchange with Jesus for grace, mercy, love, healing, and forgiveness from sin?

Devotion 2

DISCUSSION NOTES

VERSE STUDY

Matthew 6:33-34 (NIV), "But seek first his kingdom and his righteousness, and all these things will be given to you as well. Therefore do not worry about tomorrow, for tomorrow will worry about itself. Each day has enough trouble of its own."

1. How often do you find yourself worrying about something that hasn't even happened? What do you worry about the most? _____
   _____
   _____
   _____
   _____
   _____

2. Jesus tells us that today has enough trouble of its own, so we should not be adding tomorrow's trouble to our worries as well. Can you see how doing this leads to a negative outlook on life? List some of the ways this behavior negatively affects you.
   _____
   _____
   _____
   _____

Devotion 2

3. In this scripture, Jesus wants us to break the pattern of worry in our lives and turn our focus toward His kingdom instead. He uses the word *first* to tell us that His kingdom is priority over everything else, and when we put Him *first*, we don't have to worry, because He has everything we need. Why do you think this is so hard for us to do? Why do you think putting His kingdom *first* in our lives is so important?

4. What are some ways you can begin to seek God's kingdom *first* and break the pattern of worry in your life today?

SCRIPTURE REFERENCES

Matthew 6:25 (NIV), "Do not worry."

Matthew 11:28-30 (NIV), "Come to me, all you who are weary and burdened, and I will give you rest. Take my yoke upon you and learn from me, for I am gentle and humble in heart, and you will find rest for your souls. For my yoke is easy and my burden is light."

Devotion 2

CLOSING PRAYER

Father God, we thank You for Your Son, Jesus, who came to make the exchange for us. I no longer want to carry the burdens of _____

_____

_____

_. I want to put my hope in You. I do not want to worry anymore, but I choose to trust that You will take care of me. I put my hope in You; please come and renew my strength. I choose to exchange my heavy burden with You for Your yoke that is light. Teach me how to soar on wings like eagles, and lead and guide me in all Your truth, that the trials and tribulations of this world will not weigh me down. I receive Your grace, mercy, and love. Please forgive me of all my sins and restore me inside and out with Your healing touch, in Jesus' name. Amen.

Finding Strength

PERSONAL PRAYER NOTES

Devotion 3
LETTING GO

No longer are we supposed to carry around the baggage of life. Instead, we need to let go of it and give it to God, and say, "I trust You with my life and receive Your mercy for my failures and mistakes." When we continue to carry our mistakes and failures around with us, it is an act of not fully accepting what Jesus Christ did for us. We can't receive His grace completely without letting go and repenting. Repenting of our mistakes and failures humbles us to admit that we need Him and His forgiveness. The wonderful thing about repentance is that our God will not hold our sin over our heads or use it against us. It's quite the opposite. In Psalm 103:12 (NIV), we learn that "as far as the east is from the west, so far has he removed our transgressions from us." Meaning, His grace is sufficient for our shortcomings; just as it says in 2 Corinthians 12:9 (NIV), "My grace is sufficient for you, for my power is made perfect in weakness." This scripture is our breath of fresh air. We live life with high expectations for ourselves to be perfect. We want to look perfect, act perfect, and be perfect, and this unattainable goal causes us to strive for something that does not exist. We wear ourselves out trying to "be perfect." In this verse, God reminds us that this is unrealistic, and He knows it; therefore, He has made a way for us to live in His grace. When we live in His grace and let go of trying to be perfect, His power is made perfect in our weakness and our acknowledgment of who He is and of our need for Him. Our need for Him goes beyond just His forgiveness for our sins; it includes healing for our losses and broken-heartedness, and the redemption of a lost soul. To be free, we need to trust Him to lead us and protect us going forward, and in return we receive His strength for the journey. Psalm 28:7 (NIV) tells us, "The Lord is my strength and my shield; my heart trusts in him, and he helps me." Once we let go and decide to trust Him, we automatically feel lighter and can breathe better; we feel relief and even feel stronger, because we are not bringing our burdens with us. Trusting in Him means knowing we are not alone, because we have partnered with Christ as our source of strength. He comes in to pick us up and lift our heads. We can look to the future with the hope that in our next time of struggle, He is there.

Letting go can encompass more than just choosing to leave our past behind us. Isaiah 43:18-19 (NIV) tells us, "Forget the former things; do not dwell on the past.

See, I am doing a new thing! Now it springs up; do you not perceive it? I am making a way in the wilderness and streams in the wasteland." I love it when God is specific with His instructions for us. He instructs us to first forget the former things—the past, which encompasses the old way of doing things, the old mindset of how we see things, and the old way of how we respond to our circumstances. Everything must change! This includes thinking about what happened, the *whys* and the *ifs* of our past. When we choose to change, He encourages us to see from a new perspective. We cannot see from a new perspective by doing things the old way. We will not be able to see the "new thing" God is doing or be able to "perceive it" if we continue to dwell on the past. He does not say that our circumstances have changed yet, but He is making a way for us in our current wilderness and bringing streams forth in the wasteland we have found ourselves in.

This is where our perspective begins to shift from fear to trust, sadness to delight, and weakness to strength. We are no longer left alone to our own devices that have so often caused us more pain and suffering. We are on a new path, being led by our Savior, Jesus Christ, the one true source for all we need, and we can take that next step from a place of strength and not weakness. Our new outlook is described in 2 Corinthians 12:10 (NIV), "That is why, for Christ's sake, I delight in weaknesses, in insults, in hardships, in persecutions, in difficulties. For when I am weak, then I am strong." No longer will we fear that our trials will overwhelm us and take us down, but instead we can find delight in admitting to ourselves that we cannot handle it on our own, and that He is our strength. We were not meant to go through life alone. We were meant to live our lives with Him leading the way.

Devotion 3

BIBLE STUDY 3

We need to recognize that we are not meant to live life alone. Living life alone tends to create an environment of no trust, fear, and self-sufficiency. All of which leads to a life with no source of grace, peace to withstand the trials, and strength to fight the good fight of faith. Letting go of living life alone means we are choosing to partner up with Christ as our Savior and our source of all we will ever need. As we accept Jesus Christ as our Savior, He takes away our burdens and pain and becomes our first choice for all we need. In 2 Corinthians 12:9-10, weakness is not described as a negative trait, but as an opportunity for God to step into the situation and move.

DISCUSSION QUESTIONS

1. What weaknesses do you see as opportunities for God to move in your life?

2. How does grace encourage us to continue to pursue walking with Christ, even when we fail?

3. Letting go of our burdens completely changes our perspective of our personal circumstance, not the circumstance itself; but a change in perspective can move us from fear to trust, sadness to delight, and weakness to strength. What change in perspective is God making in your life today?

Devotion 3

DISCUSSION NOTES

Finding Strength

VERSE STUDY

2 Corinthians 12:9-10 (NIV), "But he said to me, 'My grace is sufficient for you, for my power is made perfect in weakness.' …That is why, for Christ's sake, I delight in weaknesses, in insults, in hardships, in persecutions, in difficulties. For when I am weak, then I am strong."

1. Jesus tells us that His grace is sufficient for us to remind us that perfection is not what He is after. He is after our surrender and recognition of who He is in our lives. How often do we find it hard to admit our weakness, failures, and mistakes? Why do you think we try so hard to hide these? _____

   _____
   _____
   _____
   _____
   _____

2. The minute we admit our weakness and failures is the minute God's grace can come in and work in our lives. He doesn't want us to admit our shortcomings so that He can put us down; rather, He waits for us to admit to them, because in doing

Devotion 3

so we admit we need an Almighty God to step into our lives. What are some shortcomings that you want to admit to so that God can step in and become "perfect in our weakness"? _____

_____
_____
_____
_____
_____
_____

3. When we recognize the need for grace and fully accept it, then when we face trials and hardships in life, we don't have to feel ashamed. We can delight in the fact that our God will be lifted up in our lives through our weaknesses and trials. How does this change your personal perspective from being weak to being strong in Christ? List some examples. _____

_____
_____
_____
_____
_____

4. What areas in your life is God speaking to you to let go of, so His power can be made perfect in

your areas of weakness? Are you willing to surrender those over to Him today? _____

_____

_____

_____

_____

_____

Devotion 3

SCRIPTURE REFERENCES

Philippians 4:6 (NIV), "Do not be anxious about anything, but in every situation, by prayer and petition, with thanksgiving, present your requests to God."

Proverbs 3:5-6 (NIV), "Trust in the Lord with all your heart and lean not on your own understanding; in all your ways submit to him, and he will make your paths straight."

CLOSING PRAYER

Father God, I thank You for setting me free of all my burdens, chains, and fears. I accept You, Jesus, as my source of grace, forgiveness, and peace. Use my weaknesses to make opportunities for You to work in my life to draw me closer to You. I put my trust in You to lead me through my circumstances. I will not be anxious but bring _____ to You in prayer. I know that my circumstances may not have changed, but my perspective is new. I will set my eyes on You and keep my hope in You to be my strength and my shield. I know that I am not alone, because You are with me. My heart trusts in You to help me, in Jesus' name. Amen.

Devotion 3

PERSONAL PRAYER NOTES

Devotion 4

RENEWED

God knows there will be trials, hardships, and difficulties in our lives that we will have to walk through. He knows that life isn't fair and there is evil in this world. That is why He has made a way for us through His Son, Jesus Christ. As we receive Jesus Christ to save us, and we confess Him as Lord over our lives, we can go forward with a new perspective. Isaiah 41:10 (NIV) tells us, "So do not fear, for I am with you; do not be dismayed, for I am your God." Fear should no longer have a hold on us, because God is with us. Where before, in times of trouble, instead of feeling secure in God we would begin to exclude ourselves and feel we didn't want to burden others with our feelings or life's trials. The good news is that God is with us through the dark times, to be our comfort and to calm our fears. Sometimes just getting out of bed feels like an impossible task, and hiding feels like the best option, but only if we choose not to accept our source of strength in Him. We must change our perspective from seeing ourselves as alone to standing strong because we have an Almighty God by our side, with a limitless supply of strength, courage, hope, peace, joy, patience, and love. This is everything we need to give us that burst of confidence to just take that first step.

Instead of feeling unable, we see ourselves as capable, just as it's written in Philippians 4:13 (NIV), "I can do all this through him who gives me strength." We are also encouraged in Psalm 46:1 (NIV) that "God is our refuge and strength, an ever-present help in trouble." A refuge is a place of protection, a place to run to for shelter and safety. In addition to having an awesome God with us, He provides a place, an atmosphere of protection. He is our safety net, which means we no longer feel afraid. When life beats us up and breaks us down, we can run to God for a place to recover and to heal. He knows exactly what we are facing and what we need, because He is our Shepherd. Psalm 23:3 (NIV) explains to us how "He refreshes [our] soul," and "He guides [us] along the right paths," and even though we are still walking through the difficulty of life, we won't be afraid, because He is with us. It is nice to have our friends there to comfort and support us when we are troubled and experiencing hardships, but they really can't fix our problems for us, heal us, or even restore us from what has already been done. The only friend who can do this is Jesus. When we run to Him and take advantage of who He is, He will dry our tears, He will bring true comfort and peace, He will heal our hearts as we stay in His presence, and He will restore our soul deep down, where it has been damaged.

While we are surrounded by our "enemies" in life, He continues to "prepare a table before [us]" (v. 5) so we can be filled and provided for as He heals and renews us. This kind of renewal is more than just a "trip to the spa" or a "getaway"; this is a deep work that occurs from living in His presence. His work isn't a "quick fix" or superficial. His work is life-changing and meant to create us into who He calls us to be. When He is our Shepherd, He calls us His own and He walks us through life, all the while taking care of our every need. We all need the Shepherd, but for so long we have lived on our own and tried to do it all in our strength, never realizing that He was there, waiting. As we stay and follow Him, He will take us off the broken and rough path we are on and lift us up and place us on His path of righteousness. He will anoint us with His oil that will soothe us and fill our spirits to a place where we will begin to overflow into others. His anointing oil renews not just our wounds but our minds to a place of belonging, wholeness, and hope. As the chapter ends in Psalm 23:6 (NIV), our perspective after spending time with our God, our Shepherd, is changed: "Surely your goodness and love will follow me all the days of my life, and I will dwell in the house of the Lord forever." We have moved to a place of life, love, and safety under His care. This isn't a temporary living arrangement; this is permanent and a place we will not want to leave: under our Shepherd's care all the days of our lives, and even until eternity, to dwell with Him forever.

Devotion 1

BIBLE STUDY 4

Renewal is a process that occurs over time as we choose to live under the Shepherd's care. It is a step-by-step process that only He knows, based on our individual experiences, trials, and hardships. He knows our highs and lows in life, the tears we have cried; not even one of our friends could ever know every detail of every emotion we have felt. It is only when we choose to walk with Christ that the process of renewal can begin. It is a choice to make a lifestyle change of living in surrender to Him. One where we follow, and He leads us to our places of rest, refuge, and provision. In these places He will dry our tears, soothe our minds, and heal our wounds by His love. Through His great love, we are comforted and will not be afraid in our new place of dwelling with Him.

Finding Strength

SCRIPTURE REFERENCES AND DISCUSSION QUESTIONS

1. Read Psalm 23 (New International Version).

2. As you read the process of the Shepherd caring for His sheep individually, answer the following questions:

    a. What are the benefits of having a Shepherd?
    b. What areas of renewal do you need in your life? (This may be physical, mental, emotional, spiritual, etc...)

3. As the Shepherd leads His sheep to places of rest and refuge, this can also be a church body, a small Bible study group of fellow believers, elders, leaders, and/or pastors whom God can use to help this process of renewal take place.

    c. Are you a part of a church body? Do you have a group of Christian believers in your life whom you can go to for guidance?
    d. If not, becoming a part of a Christian church body will encourage this new lifestyle of dwelling with the Shepherd.

Devotion 1

DISCUSSION NOTES

Finding Strength

VERSE STUDY

Proverbs 3:5-6 (NIV), "Trust in the Lord with all your heart and lean not on your own understanding; in all your ways submit to him, and he will make your paths straight."

1. What does the phrase "lean not on your own understanding" mean to you in this verse? _____

   _____
   _____
   _____
   _____
   _____

2. How many times do we tend to try to figure out life on our own before we go to God for help? Can you think of some times in your life where this has been the case, and things did not work out for the best? _____

   _____
   _____
   _____
   _____

3. Having Jesus as our Shepherd to trust in eliminates our personal efforts of figuring out which direction we are meant to walk in, requires us to submit our personal ideas and agendas, and causes

Devotion 4

us to follow His lead. It's not about following our heart, but following His heart. What personal ideas and agendas do you have that need to be submitted to the Lord? _____

_____
_____
_____
_____
_____

4. A good shepherd always has the good of the flock in mind. The shepherd also knows the lay of the land better, where the dangerous terrain is, and how to protect his flock from predators. Our good Shepherd, Jesus, knows the world and all its traps and danger areas to avoid better than we do. He also knows our weaknesses and how to care for us when we are wounded and tired. In His goodness, He brings us to places of rest and renewal. How does having such a wonderful Shepherd over your life make you feel about your current situation and future? _____

_____
_____
_____
_____
_____

CLOSING PRAYER

Father God, thank You for being a good Shepherd to Your people. Thank You for calling me one of Your own. You are so loving and caring, and You see my hurts and pains and know exactly what I need. I surrender myself to Your ways; lead me to places of rest and refuge in my life. Begin the process of renewal in my heart, mind, and soul. Fill me with Your love and goodness so that I may be restored and whole, and remove anything from me that hinders my walk with You or takes me astray. I want to dwell in the house of the Lord forever and ever. Amen.

Devotion 1

PERSONAL PRAYER NOTES

Devotion 5

DAILY PORTION

The time of the day when I feel the most struggle is in the morning. The minute that I get up, my mind begins to go over various situations in my head that I know I will face. It causes me to contemplate how I am going to get through the day. I literally have to just stop and ask the Lord to help me get through the day and give Him everything I am worried about. The wonderful thing about leaning on the Lord and trusting Him is that it takes the stress off me and stops the negative cycle of worrying. I get myself up for the day, knowing I've put everything in His hands. The struggles we face will try to keep us down and keep us from moving forward in life. For many, the struggles build up, leading to depression and anxiety which make it almost impossible to do anything. Leaving us debilitated and ineffective in our lives. This is why it is so important to have the realization that God is our daily portion. He is the daily provision for what we need to keep us going. When we don't acknowledge Him we can't receive our provision, and we are left feeling helpless, weak, and inadequate. Accepting Christ as our

Savior, as our source, our Shepherd, and allowing Him to begin to heal our hearts does not mean the struggle will necessarily stop; instead of being discouraged that our circumstances haven't changed, we choose to take God at His word. The choice is ours. God will not force His way into our lives; each day the choice is ours to make.

When we choose Him, we are not alone in facing the day. In Deuteronomy 31:8 (NIV) we are reassured, "The Lord himself goes before you and will be with you; he will never leave you nor forsake you. Do not be afraid; do not be discouraged." These words of encouragement are life-giving to us and will help us have hope from the start of our day until it ends. Usually, during a time of trouble we can find support from our family and friends, but once the dust settles, they are busy or can't fully understand our emotions, and we can feel alone again. God is never too busy for us or out of reach, and He always understands what we feel. It is we who put ourselves out of reach of Him and think it's okay to exclude and isolate ourselves. This harms us even more, because it separates us from God, leaving us feeling empty without our daily provision. To make sure we do not make this mistake, we must daily "look to the Lord and his strength; seek his face always" (1 Chronicles 16:11 NIV).

This new way of living with Jesus Christ is a relationship; it is a two-way street where we live with Him and put our focus on Him daily. It isn't just a one-time moment where we acknowledge Him and from then on, we have it all. Yes, we have accepted His invitation, and His offer will never be taken back from us, but this offer we have accepted is to have a relationship with Him. It is a process of learning who He is and who we are because of Him. As we grow in the knowledge of who He is to us, we discover that He has more for us than we could ever know. We can begin by calling on Him daily, as in Isaiah 33:2 (NIV), "Lord, be gracious to us; we long for you. Be our strength every morning, our salvation in time of distress." Every morning, we are encouraged to ask Him to be strong in our lives to receive our daily provision. God wants us to call upon His name daily, because He knows that when we try to take each day of our own accord, we deplete ourselves, and we lose sight of Him. When we truly become dependent on Him, we naturally will return to Him every day and live from a place of limitless supply.

The prayer Jesus taught us to pray encourages us all to ask for daily provision. "Give us today our daily bread" (Matthew 6:11 NIV). In coming to the Lord daily, we are demonstrating our trust and faith in God to provide for our needs. When we do not put our trust in Him, it allows for unbelief and worry to set in. Jesus teaches us, "Therefore do not worry about tomorrow, for tomorrow will worry about itself" in Matthew 6:34 (NIV). Jesus describes the faithfulness of God in Matthew 6:26 to provide food, shelter, and clothing for His creation daily. Why then should we worry; will He not do the same for us? Our efforts to control and worry about our daily needs are not a testament of our faith in Him. It is when we choose not to worry, and spend time focusing on Him, that we do what He is asking of us. We are following His Word and exercising our faith when we pray for His daily provision. Daily, we accept the invitation to be in full relationship with our Savior and everything He has for us by calling on His name to be who He has said He is in our life.

BIBLE STUDY 5

We now have a new perspective: to live with a daily awareness of who God is in our lives and to know that He does not change, despite our circumstances or worries. He is always the same. We cannot forget to take Him at His word. We cannot forget to receive the gifts of strength, provision, and love He freely gives to His people. This is the benefit of being in right relationship with our heavenly Father. Every day we ask Him to give us our daily bread, and we acknowledge that He is the ultimate provider in every circumstance and that we need Him. In needing Him, we see that we are meant to live life with Him, and in doing so we will live more and abundantly.

DISCUSSION QUESTIONS

1. When do you feel the struggles of the day are most overwhelming?

2. Have these struggles affected your ability to get through your day?

3. Do you recognize the importance of calling on the Lord in those very moments to bring you strength?

4. Praying the "Our Father" every morning can be instrumental in setting the tone and atmosphere of your day and in putting a stop to the devil's plans to derail you.

5. Where would you rate your relationship with Jesus today?

Devotion 5

DISCUSSION NOTES

Finding Strength

VERSE STUDY

Psalm 34:8 (NIV), "Taste and see that the Lord is good; blessed is the one who takes refuge in him."

1. Our senses of taste and sight are very powerful. They provide us not just with information about what is right in front of us, but they also help us to process and perceive an environment or a mood, and to create a knowledge base of likes and dislikes to improve upon or avoid in the future. In this scripture, "taste and see" is a directive for us to fully experience the Lord so we can know for ourselves how good He is. When you taste or see something incredible, it changes your opinion and idea of it. Do you feel you have fully experienced how good the Lord is in this way? Give an example. _____

    _____

    _____

    _____

    _____

2. Many times, people don't like to try something new, and they pass on new tastes and adventures in life because of past opinions and ideas that they

Devotion 5

have developed themselves or from others. Once we experience the goodness of God, there is no turning back. What is one way you can express what it means to you to "taste and see that the Lord is good" to someone who has not been able to experience Him? _____

_____
_____
_____
_____
_____

3. When we have had the opportunity to fully experience the Lord in this way, we realize that His goodness is not just an occasional, chance meeting. It is meant to be a daily encounter that blesses us. The Lord never keeps us at an arm's length away. He wants us to know Him and find refuge in Him. Are you taking advantage and finding refuge in the Lord? Do you run to Him for safety from the day-to-day and trials you face? If you do, explain how, and if you don't, why not? _____

_____
_____
_____
_____

4. Our daily provision from the Lord includes "tasting and seeing" His goodness. What are some ways you can begin to daily experience that the Lord is good? _____

Devotion 5

SCRIPTURE REFERENCES

Read the "Our Father" in Matthew 6:9-13.

John 10:10 (NIV), "The thief comes only to steal and kill and destroy; I have come that they may have life, and have it to the full."

CLOSING PRAYER

Heavenly Father, You are greater and able to save me from any circumstance that I may find myself in. I call upon Your name daily to be my provision, my forgiveness, my guide, to keep me from temptation and deliver me from all evil. I want to know You more and live to help bring Your kingdom into my life. I choose to trust You, and I break the cycle of worry in my life, because I know You have everything I need. I will seek Your face and Your ways daily, that I may know more of You and Your plans for my life, in Jesus' name. Amen.

Devotion 5

PERSONAL PRAYER NOTES

Devotion 6

STRENGTH TO ENDURE

Each day comes with its own struggles, and we now know that God is our daily portion, but the days and nights can be long for many of us. David describes in his prayer, "Weeping may endure for a night, but joy comes in the morning" (Psalm 30:5 NKJV). Waiting for our morning to come is not easy to do, but we are called to endure. Romans 5:3-5 (ESV), "Not only that, but we rejoice in our sufferings, knowing that suffering produces endurance, and endurance produces character, and character produces hope, and hope does not put us to shame, because God's love has been poured into our hearts through the Holy Spirit who has been given to us." Be encouraged to know that our sufferings are being used to bring growth while His Holy Spirit fills our hearts with His love. The Lord knows the struggles that we face will be difficult, and sometimes long and trying, but He also sees the end from the beginning, meaning our character and our trust in Him after we've arrived on the other side of our situation. "The proof is in the pudding," so to speak. It is disappointing when we see others completely broken, weak, cold-hearted, angry, or living in fear after they have been through an ordeal, but God is telling us that this does not have to be the case for us. Our journey, though it requires endurance to see it through, will not get the best of us. We just have to press through and endure with His perspective and the hope that He gives. We cannot get weary in welldoing, because the reward is great. "And let us not grow weary while doing good, for in due season we shall reap if we do not lose heart" (Galatians 6:9 NKJV). Doing good while going through trials seems impossible at times, but not when we have a Shepherd who dries our tears, binds up our wounds, and protects us in the dark places. This is a life process, and we need to stay encouraged, keep our eyes on Him, and endure as we stay on the path God has for us.

This journey, though it may seem long, is for our benefit. What a blessing it is to learn to trust God as our daily source as we endure the difficult days and nights, and to be set free from the bondages of worry, loss, depression, anger, and hopelessness. Let the Lord use this process to change your perspective from loss to gain. "Consider it pure joy, my brothers and sisters, whenever you face trials of many kinds, because you know that the testing of your faith produces perseverance" (James 1:2-3 NIV). *Perseverance* is the continued effort to accomplish or do something despite difficulties, failure, or opposition. Perseverance requires endurance, the stamina to not stop the effort, throughout the entire life process. We all know life is difficult, some seasons more than others, but how many times have we come out on the other side of it and said to ourselves, "Thank God I never gave up." Our perseverance is what helps us wake up and continue to work through our day and night and then do it all over again the next day, despite failure or change in our circumstances. This is the character of God that has been brought forth out of us, and though it is tiring, we have been given the strength of God to not quit.

Being patient with an attitude of doing good as we wait for the breakthrough to come produces character. Then the more we will recognize that we can be overcomers in Christ, and hope will arise. This brings about maturity in our walk with the Lord. Our ability to understand this and trust Him in the process gives us strength to endure. This means that our relationship with Him has grown, because while going through this process we have developed a history of trust. We know we can trust that He will provide all that we need when we need it. James 1:4 (NIV), "Let perseverance finish its work so that you may be mature and complete, not lacking anything." Our walk with the Lord requires growth to see from His perspective and to see past our circumstances to where we are living victoriously over our situation. God's goal for us is not to just get by in life, but to be made whole in Him. He wants us to be mature in the knowledge of who He is and who we are in Him.

Devotion 6

BIBLE STUDY 6

Endurance is the ability to keep going, without giving in to our weaknesses that will cause us to quit. Perseverance is the effort to finish despite our difficulties, failure, or opposition. These skills are not automatic; they come from a place of maturity in our lives. When you first begin to learn a craft or sport, endurance and perseverance aren't usually evident. They are developed over time and through continual practice. As we see these skills developed, the ability to endure when tested improves, because we don't give in as soon as it gets hard. This reminds me of the scripture, "And let us not grow weary while doing good, for in due season we shall reap if we do not lose heart" (Galatians 6:9 NKJV). In life, we must continue to do good, have a positive demeanor, and speak life into our circumstance. This may sound difficult, to be in a good mood through a trial, but not with God. Our attitude comes from a place of who God is, and not what we see around us. This means we press through, even when we don't see the changes we are expecting when we expect them; even more, He fills us with His love and hope by His Holy Spirit. We need to continue to follow God's plan for our lives, no matter what. Our harvest is the breakthrough we are looking for: the plan and purpose that God has for our lives.

DISCUSSION QUESTIONS

1. What do you feel is the most difficult to endure in your situation?

2. Can you see how with each obstacle you face, your ability to endure increases a little more with the help of God and is evidence of your growing maturity as a follower of Christ?

3. Perseverance builds character, but not just any character: the character of God in us.

4. What are some ways you can practice doing good throughout your circumstance?

Devotion 6

DISCUSSION NOTES

Finding Strength

VERSE STUDY

1 Corinthians 9:24-27 (NIV), "Do you not know that in a race all the runners run, but only one gets the prize? Run in such a way as to get the prize. Everyone who competes in the games goes into strict training. They do it to get a crown that will not last, but we do it to get a crown that will last forever. Therefore I do not run like someone running aimlessly; I do not fight like a boxer beating the air. No, I strike a blow to my body and make it my slave so that after I have preached to others, I myself will not be disqualified for the prize."

1. We have our own race to run in life and are encouraged to run with a goal in mind: to finish strong. How do you see yourself doing so far? Explain. _____
   _____
   _____
   _____
   _____

2. Our race to run is long and requires us to go the distance, but without any training our endurance will not be enough to finish the race. The Holy

Devotion 6

Spirit has been sent to be our "trainer" to give guidance, support, and comfort during our journey through life. Can you recognize certain times in your life where the Holy Spirit has tried to give you some training and direction, or a warning for what's coming ahead? How did you respond? ___

_____
_____
_____
_____
_____

3. We have been given instruction not to run "aimlessly" or without a goal in mind, because then what we do will be of no effect; it is as though we are just going through the motions. The type of "training" we need requires self-discipline. When we have a goal and a direction from the Holy Spirit on how to complete this leg of the race, we need to have self-discipline to make sure it happens. What areas of self-discipline do you feel the Holy Spirit has been speaking to you about in order to be more effective? _____

_____
_____

_____

_____

_____

4. We know that training with self-discipline will help us endure the trials we face in life. We can't just go through the motions; we all have been given a purpose and a call by God. What purpose have you been given to keep running your race?

_____

_____

_____

_____

_____

_____

Devotion 6

SCRIPTURE REFERENCES

Romans 5:3-5 and Galatians 6:9

These two verses go hand in hand. For perseverance, character, and hope to be developed in us, we need to not get weary in doing good throughout our trials and hardships. If we give in to anger and frustration, the character of God will not be fully developed, and our breakthrough will be hindered from happening.

Hebrews 10:36 (NIV), "You need to persevere so that when you have done the will of God, you will receive what he has promised."

Perseverance to follow God's plan for our lives brings us to His promises.

CLOSING PRAYER

Father God, I know that You want me to continue the process of walking with You and growing in my relationship with You. I know that this does not mean that all trials and hardships in my life will stop, but that when they do come, You are with me. Give me the strength to persevere and endure until the breakthrough comes. Let perseverance build character in me, that hope may arise out of my circumstances. Lord, give me strength, that I may not grow weary in doing good as I follow Your Word and obey Your plans for my life, in Jesus' name. Amen.

Devotion 6

PERSONAL PRAYER NOTES

Devotion 7
STRENGTH IN THE PROMISE

Learning to persevere and endure the good fight of faith is not without its reward. Hebrews 10:36 (NIV), "You need to persevere so that when you have done the will of God, you will receive what he has promised." The good news is that His promises are not empty words spoken in a moment of emotion, but God's promises are forever! Today, promises are not what they used to be. Many times, we are reminded of all the broken promises that others have made and that we have made as well. The difference is that our God never breaks His promises to us, because He cannot go against His own Word. 2 Corinthians 1:20 (NIV), "For no matter how many promises God has made, they are 'Yes' in Christ. And so through him the 'Amen' is spoken by us to the glory of God." We must reflect upon the promises God has made to us and stand firm on what His Word declares for our lives. When we stand on His promises, we are encouraged and strengthened to keep going. His promises are worth holding on to.

We have already received our first promise when

we accepted Jesus as our Lord and Savior. 1 John 2:25 (NIV), "And this is what he promised us—eternal life." We don't have to wait to receive this promise of eternal life. It has already been given to us. We know where we are going and know this life does not end here. We have a place with the Father, because we now belong to Him. This is good news, and we can hold on to it from here until eternity. This is what it means to have the hope of glory, to be with Him, united for all eternity. You may think that will be too far away, but meanwhile, He has also given us the promise that He will be with us always. "The Lord himself goes before you and will be with you; he will never leave you nor forsake you. Do not be afraid; do not be discouraged" (Deuteronomy 31:8 NIV). We know this is a promise, because He speaks it several times to us in 1 Kings, Joshua, and Hebrews. This is a promise to reassure us that we don't have to be afraid, because He is there taking care of us every step of the way. Jesus always secures His promises through His Word, which is why we must meditate on His words day and night. Psalm 1:2 (NKJV), "But his delight is in the law of the Lord, and in His law he meditates day and night." Meditating on the Word of God brings encouragement and reminds us of the goodness of God, and this brings us joy. Our reading His Word and promises is like a bride reading her bridegroom's love letters.

We can meditate and "replay" the words the Father has spoken to us by reading and hearing His words. Reading the Bible daily teaches us who God is and what He says about us. In His Word, He reveals who we are in Him and what He will do for us. This is the key to building up our faith in the Lord. Romans 10:17 (NKJV), "So then faith comes by hearing, and hearing by the word of God." We reinforce our relationship with the Lord and secure the foundation we have established through these devotions of *Finding Strength* by continuing to read His Word.

The devotions in *Finding Strength* are only the beginning. They have brought us to finding Jesus and renewing our relationship with Him as our source for all that we need. He is the God we can trust to be our everything. My prayer and hope are that through this devotional series, you have come to know the Lord Jesus as your Savior and have chosen to receive Him completely. Each devotion draws you closer to Him through an understanding that we are not meant to live life in our own strength, but through the power of Jesus Christ. Only in this way will we know who we truly are and experience Jesus. Acts 17:28 (NKJV), "For in Him we live and move and have our being." This journey is not over; God has so much more for each one of us. May the Lord continue this work and reveal Himself to us more and more "to make her holy, cleansing her by the washing with water through the word" (Ephesians 5:26 NIV).

Devotion 7

BIBLE STUDY 7

A promise does not carry the same weight it used to in today's world. Everywhere we look, we can see promises being made and then broken as quickly as they were given. This is not the case for us and our deep relationship with Christ. He assures us with His words throughout all generations that His promises do not change, and He is the same yesterday, today, and forever. We need to meditate on His Word to continue the work that has already been done in our hearts and to reinforce the ground that has been taken. A beautiful picture of our journey through this devotional is perfectly summarized in Isaiah 61:3 (NKJV), "To console those who mourn in Zion, to give them beauty for ashes, the oil of joy for mourning, the garment of praise for the spirit of heaviness; that they may be called trees of righteousness, the planting of the Lord, that He may be glorified." God has comforted us during our troubles, wiped our tears, and became our Shepherd. He has anointed us with His oil and has taken away all our burdens in exchange for His garments that bring us praise and joy. We are now beautiful and planted in His strong foundation, with roots connected to a limitless supply of His provision. Amen!

DISCUSSION QUESTIONS

1. Have you experienced a broken promise in your life recently?

2. Do you find it hard to trust again?

3. Can you see how God upholds His promises to us through His Word?

4. Throughout this devotion, what have been the most significant revelations you have received?

Devotion 7

DISCUSSION NOTES

Finding Strength

VERSE STUDY

Hebrews 10:23-25 (NIV), "Let us hold unswervingly to the hope we profess, for he who promised is faithful. And let us consider how we may spur one another on toward love and good deeds, not giving up meeting together, as some are in the habit of doing, but encouraging one another—and all the more as you see the Day approaching."

1. Our God does not make broken promises to us. We can read above that He is faithful to keep His promises. In return, we must hold on "unswervingly" to our newfound hope in Him. What does the word *unswervingly* mean to you regarding how we are to hold on to the promises of God?

   _____
   _____
   _____
   _____
   _____
   _____

2. Our relationship with our Lord and Savior does not stop with just us and Him. It is meant to be a starting point for us to share the good news with

Devotion 7

others. Just as we have been encouraged by Him, we are meant to encourage others in their places of difficulty. What are some ways you can "spur one another on toward love and good deeds"? ___

_____
_____
_____
_____
_____

3. Our journey is a process of growing and becoming more mature in the character of Christ. We can't do this alone. This is a lifestyle change for many of us. List some areas of your life where you can improve. _____

_____
_____
_____
_____
_____

4. At the end of these verses, it mentions that we are to continue living this way, "and all the more as you see the Day approaching." This means we are not to stop and say "I've done enough; that's as

much as I'm going to do." On the contrary, until the Lord returns, we are to continue in encouraging one another and meeting together. We cannot give up in pursuing Him. Does this change the view you have for your Christian walk in the future? How? _____

_____

_____

_____

_____

_____

Devotion 7

SCRIPTURE REFERENCES

1 John 2:24-25

It is important for us to remember the promise of God

-for example, in a marriage, the husband and wife wear wedding bands as reminders of the vows made

The Lord is telling us here to make sure the words He has spoken to us remain in us

Furthermore, that we stand in the new place He has put us (in the Son and the Father)

We are on the receiving end of the promises of God, but if we forget His words and what they mean to us, we can lose hope, faith, and trust in Him

> Therefore, we need to build our faith by hearing the Word of God

> Continuing to hear the Word of God encourages us to remain in the place of promise

Here are some ways you can plan to continue to grow and keep yourself in the place of His promises:
- Reading the Bible

- Bible study/devotionals
- Fellowship with Christ
- Prayer
- Worship
- Attending church to fellowship with others

What are some of the ways you plan to continue your relationship with Christ?

_____

_____

_____

_____

_____

_____

_____

_____

_____

CLOSING PRAYER

Lord, I thank You for Your promises. You are a good God who will never change Your mind. You are the same yesterday, today, and forever. I choose to meditate on Your words and keep myself in the place of promise by

_____

___ _____

_____. In this place of promise, You are my source of strength. I choose daily to surrender all my cares and worries to You, and I will trust You for all I need. Be my Shepherd, and lead and guide me to places of rest, renewal, and peace. Let the character of God be developed in me to full maturity as I persevere and endure to receive my breakthrough for

_____ _____

_____. I now know that I am meant to live with You and not alone. Thank You, Jesus, for giving me a new perspective about who You are to me. I love You, Jesus. In Jesus' name, let Your will be done in my life, I pray. Amen.

Finding Strength

PERSONAL PRAYER NOTES

www.ingramcontent.com/pod-product-compliance
Lightning Source LLC
LaVergne TN
LVHW011207190225
804019LV00003B/5